Flying into the Wind

North Warwickshire College of Technology & Art
Hinckley Road,
Nuneaton

by **David Leland**

Editor **Paul Kelley**
The Television Literacy Project

Contents

Cambridge University Press
Cambridge
London   New York   New Rochelle
Melbourne   Sydney

Tales out of School
Birth of a Nation
Flying into the Wind
Rhino
Made in Britain

Published by the Press Syndicate of the University of Cambridge
The Pitt Building, Trumpington Street, Cambridge CB2 1RP
32 East 57th Street, New York, NY 10022, USA
10 Stamford Road, Oakleigh, Melbourne 3166, Australia

First published 1985
Third printing 1987

Printed in Great Britain at the University Press, Cambridge

ISBN 0 521 31373 2

DS

A videocassette of this film is available to schools and
colleges from the following British suppliers. (Please check
for prices at the time of ordering.)

Cambridge University Press
(Home Sales Department)
The Edinburgh Building
Shaftesbury Road
Cambridge CB2 2RU

Concord Films Council Ltd
201 Felixstowe Road
Ipswich
Suffolk IP3 9BJ
(Videocassettes are also available for hire.)

The Guild Organisation Ltd
Oundle Road
Peterborough PE2 9PZ
(Videocassettes are also available for hire.)

Introduction

This is the second in a quartet of films written for Central Independent Television. This quartet of films started with a conversation between myself and Margaret Matheson, the producer of the films and, at the time, Controller of Drama at Central Television. I was already very interested in education and the general status of young people in our society. We both saw education as a major issue which affected everybody's life, yet it was not being reflected in contemporary drama.

There then followed a period of time during which I did further research into particular topics, such as juvenile crime, children in care, the curriculum in schools, and so on; while, at the same time, Margaret Matheson and I continued to discuss what each film would be about, how long they would be and what form they might take. Once decisions had been taken (four films of ninety minutes duration), I was then commissioned to write the scripts. I wrote the scripts over a period of twelve months after which they went into production. I went on to write second and third drafts of each script, the changes being born out of discussions of what I had written.

I have included some material from earlier drafts in the text printed in this volume in order to make a better reading text. The text has been printed in a way that is similar to how scripts appear, with a number and a rule across the page to indicate each new scene. For each scene there is an indication to show whether it is interior or exterior, where it is, and whether it is night or day. All this information helps others plan the production of a film. I have left out the directions at the end of scenes (such as 'fade', 'cut to', or 'dissolve') as the producer usually decides how the change from one scene to another will be done.

A script is a very incomplete form. It only has real life when it has been performed, recorded and transformed by other people into a film. For this reason, I am particularly pleased that they are to be studied in schools as both script and film.

Making a film for television

Film making is a hazardous and unpredictable process. Even though a film may begin with the words of one person, the writer, ultimately it is the product of many people all involved in a process in which no single individual has complete control. Film making is a communal art. The best way to find out about it, film or video, is to do it yourself.

It may surprise some people when I refer to *Flying into the Wind* as a 'film', and this raises an important point about how television programmes are made. Everything we see on television is recorded on either video tape or film. The same holds true for television drama. Some dramas are recorded on video tape, some on film, and some are a combination of the two mediums.

Watch any television news report and you will soon discover that the visual quality of video (newsreader in the studio) is different from that of film (on location news reports). People differ in their preference between the two mediums, often choosing to work in one rather than the other. My purpose here is not to make comparisons of merit between the two but to explain how video and film are used in the production of television drama, and how a television company prepares and makes television film drama.

In the main, dramas recorded on video tape are shot in studios with specially constructed sets.

The principle of recording drama on video tape is the same as the broadcast of a football match on *Match of the Day*. The action is covered from different angles by several cameras, and a Vision Mixer cuts from one camera viewpoint to another. What the viewer sees is an instant edited selection of several possible images. The finished result is what we see when watching a live television broadcast of a football match.

Unlike a football match, drama is rehearsed and therefore it is easier to control what happens in front of the cameras. In the studio, whole sequences are rehearsed by the actors, camera positions are fixed, and then the scene is recorded onto a master tape, each camera shot being cut together at the push of a button by the Vision Mixer from the control panel.

Anyone who has seen an outside broadcast unit in action will know that the video equipment – cameras, cables and mobile recording units – takes up a lot of space. Like a travelling circus, it's very large and difficult to move. This presents relatively few problems if the action is confined to one location (such as a concert hall or a tennis court), but with a drama where the action is usually spread across several locations, then the practical problems tend to multiply. However, as new video equipment comes into use, exciting possibilities as to how we use video are presented and are waiting to be explored.

Drama shot on film for television tends to be shot almost exclusively on location, i.e., it uses real places to locate the action as opposed to artificially constructed sets. This is not a rule and there are many exceptions – I am merely pointing out the major areas of division.

Film dramas are usually shot using only one camera. The film camera is adaptable and can be fixed to different kinds of equipment to produce different kinds of shot. It can be mounted on a tripod, on wheels, on tracks, carried by hand or mounted on giant cranes or hoists.

Film is recorded one shot at a time. For example: a wide shot will give a general, overall picture of the action rehearsed and performed by the actors; then, perhaps, close-ups of each character's actions and reactions will be shot, and so on. This means that scenes must be enacted by the performers not once but many times. It is often a long, painstaking and meticulous process, taking hours to shoot very short sequences. It requires tremendous concentration and skill from the actors and technicians to produce the required effect.

Unlike video, which has instant playback, when a sequence of action has been recorded on film, the film has to be processed – just like holiday snaps – before the results can be seen.

Sound is recorded separately but technically synchronised so that the dialogue and other sounds can be matched to the visual action of the film. This is the purpose of the clapperboard. Apart from giving a visual record of the scene and shot numbers, the actual clapper marks a visual and sound starting point to which sound and vision can be synchronised to play back in the viewing studio.

If all the shots (or rushes) of a particular sequence are strung together, what one sees is a disjointed sequence of actions, often with some of the sequence repeated several times, which makes no clear sense.

It is not until the film is literally cut up and joined together with sellotape that the action begins to make some kind of sense and resemble what we expect to see on the screen. This process is called editing and often takes up more time than the actual shooting of the film. What this process entails can easily be discovered by anybody using a Super 8 camera and simple editing equipment.

Birth of a Nation, *Flying into the Wind*, *Rhino* and *Made in Britain* were shot entirely on film and on location.

The making of a film has several basic stages of production: writing the script, pre-production, shooting the film, editing, promotion and presentation. Once a script has been written and the company makes a commitment to produce the film (in other words, is prepared to spend its money), then the film goes into pre-production.

Pre-production is an intensive period of time during which all the departments involved in the making of the film prepare for the most intensive period of all – shooting the film. The departments involved include: production department (which includes writer, director and producer, plus the location manager whose job it is to find the locations to shoot the film); the camera and sound departments; the art department, responsible for the design of the film; the wardrobe, make-up and hairdressing departments; and editing, accounts, publicity, electricians, props, construction, transport and (most important) catering. Actors are interviewed and contracted to play the parts in the script.

Shooting a film is a failsafe mission – once you start there is no going back. Each day has been carefully scheduled, each scene has only a limited period of time in which to be rehearsed and shot. Any delay costs money. Big delays may result in whole sequences having to be cut from the script or rewritten in order to fit into a new schedule. If the film is being shot outside then everybody prays for the weather to be kind.

Once a film is shot most of the crew disperse, moving on to other work, while the editor and the director get on with cutting the film. The producer and the writer often collaborate in this process; and the lighting cameraman or woman comes in to grade the colour and visual quality of the final print of the film. Then the film is ready for presentation. On average the time between the finished script and presentation – when the public sees the film – is one year.

As can be seen from this brief account of film production, a completed script is only a beginning. Having written the script, some writers want nothing to do with production, preferring to move on to new projects. Some writers would prefer to be involved in the production but are excluded or gently elbowed out of the process by the company. Other writers, having spent a lot of time researching and writing the script, wish to be part of the making of the film and are considered an essential part of the production team. Many directors and writers work closely together, interpreting, changing and rewriting the script as the shooting of the film progresses, which is, in the main, how I worked on these four films.

Education and the law

It was always my hope that the films might lead us all to question exactly what we mean when we use the word 'education', and to consider whether the system of education we have is the only one possible. These questions have been raised in a dramatic way in court when families who wish to educate their own children have tried to show that there are alternatives to school. These legal battles have highlighted many of the key issues about school in our society, and it is important to look at how the laws relating to education work.

It comes as a surprise to most people to discover that, for a child, going to school is not compulsory in Britain. Education, yes. School, no.

Section 36 of the 1944 Education Act states:

'It shall be the duty of the parent of every child of compulsory school age to cause him to receive efficient full-time education suitable to his age, ability and aptitude, either by regular attendance at school or otherwise.'

It is the 'or otherwise' which allows the parents (not the child) the legal right either to send their child to school or to devise (or search out) some alternative system of education.

Some parents have decided not to send their children to school, but to educate them at home. This is a bold and bewildering step that often leads to conflict with the authorities (as well as with friends and family, and within themselves).

The number of people involved in the de-schooling or home education movement is small, but significant. As a minority, they highlight our legal right to choose educational alternatives and challenge us to look more closely at our educational system as a whole. They lead us to ask questions.

In Britain there is the organisation 'Education Otherwise' open to help and advise anyone who is interested in de-schooling. In America, there is 'Growing Without Schooling' led by John Holt who, among his many excellent books on education, has written *Teach Your Own*, which is about home education (see 'Useful addresses').

Like parents, Education Authorities also have legal obligations to ensure that children receive a proper education. When parents do not send their children to school (for whatever reason) the Local Education Authority, after visits to the family by an Education Welfare Officer, will usually serve the parents with a school attendance order which requires the parents 'to cause the child forthwith to become a registered pupil at the school named in this order.' If the parents do not send their children to the designated school, they will be summonsed to appear at the local Magistrates Court where they will be fined and ordered, yet again, to send their children to school.

If the children still fail to attend school then it is possible (indeed probable) that the magistrates, upon the recommendation of the Authority, will order the children to be put into care. Essentially, what being 'put into care' means is that the court orders the parental rights to be transferred from the parents to the authorities – usually the Social Services. The children are removed from their homes, taken from the care of their parents, placed in a Community Home – and sent to school.

Thus parents who have taken the positive decision to educate their children outside the school system (as opposed to those parents who simply allow their children to truant) often find themselves in legal conflict with the authorities. Obviously if the parents are served with a school attendance order and they fail to send their children to school, they are guilty of not complying with the law and run the risk of having their children put into care. However, if parents can argue and prove in court that they are providing a proper education for their children, then they are within their legal right not to send their children to school:

'If any person upon whom an attendance order has been served fails to comply with the requirements of the order he shall be guilty of an offence against this section unless he proves he is causing the child to receive efficient full-time education suitable to his age, ability and aptitude otherwise than at school.'

(1944 Education Act, Section 37)

Although the Education Authority takes the preliminary steps, the decision as to whether children are receiving 'efficient full-time education' is made by the court.

It was researching precisely this kind of conflict between

9

parents and Local Education Authorities which led me to write *Flying into the Wind.* Among the various situations I researched, the script draws most particularly from an appeal case heard in the Crown Court at Worcester between the Harrison family and the Hereford and Worcester Education Authority. I would hasten to add that the film is not the story of the Harrison family, although it owes a great deal to them.

Although the Education Act requires both parents and education authorities to ensure that children receive an 'efficient full-time education suitable to his age, ability and aptitude', the Act conveniently side-steps stating exactly what it means by any of these words. The Education Act offers no definitions for such important words as 'efficient', 'full-time', 'ability', 'aptitude', or even the most fundamental word, 'education'. In the main it has been left to Education Authorities to define the meaning of the Act simply by dint of the curriculum and general regime offered in schools. This, in turn, is determined by the social and political structures of the time. The kind of education we are all caused to receive is, without doubt, a political issue.

Even though an Education Authority may not approve of the teaching methods employed by a family such as the Harrisons, or the subjects they study, or their social and political attitudes, such a family can argue in court that they are providing their children with a proper education, and this challenges the court to define the key words in the Education Act. Even though we may not choose to educate our children at home, the actions of such people are important because they question the status quo and the education system most of us take for granted.

If a law does not define its own terms, then it is common practice for a judge to look for guidance at previous cases of a similar nature. Such a case might form what is called a precedent, defining some of the terms in the law. It is hard to find precedents where cases were decided in favour of parents wanting to educate their children at home; but there is one. One parent did succeed in obtaining a judgment in favour of an entirely informal education at home: on

15 November 1961, after a ten-year struggle which included eleven court appearances, Mrs Joy Baker won her appeal against her conviction by Dereham magistrates, and the Chairman of the Norfolk Quarter Sessions Appeals Committee stated that the unorthodox education she was giving her children did satisfy the terms of the Education Act. This verdict was upheld by the Lord Chief Justice when the Norfolk Education Authority appealed to the Divisional Court; their request for leave to appeal to the House of Lords was refused. None of Mrs Baker's seven children ever went to school. (The statements made on this point in the first two printings of this book were incorrect.)

The eloquence of the evidence presented in the courts by Mrs Baker, and by the Harrisons and other families, has led to a change of attitude within many Local Education Authorities who are now more reluctant to argue the *pros* and *cons* of the education system in the public arena of the courtroom. Although the authorities may not approve of some families' methods, they may now cooperate with some families who wish to educate their children outside the school system.

There have been significant victories, then, but there is still much doubt about the validity of other kinds of education. *Flying into the Wind* is a reflection of this on-going contention.

Studying films in school

For anyone with half an interest in how we are raised and how we learn, *Flying into the Wind* raises many issues.

As a film and text to be studied it is there to be interpreted and discussed from whatever viewpoint you may care to choose. In regard to this film, as with all the others, there are no right and wrong answers. It matters not a damn if the writer is considered to be in favour of compulsory schooling or is an advocate of de-schooling (and both attitudes have been attributed to me). There will always be those critics who demand that the writer be of one persuasion or another. This attitude is born, at least in part, from the notion that there always has to be a right or a wrong answer. Personally I take the view that one may choose to be a vegetarian but still have the taste for meat.

I have visited many schools to discuss with students issues raised by the four films. It appeared to come as something of a shock to one group when I suggested that, in their lives, they were closer to being parents than pupils starting school. Having been in school for at least ten years, most would soon be leaving and, within a relatively short time, many would become parents. I suggested that we should discuss education from the perspective of parents, or prospective parents, rather than that of school pupils in the process of receiving education. It led to an excellent discussion in which we talked about our experiences at school, our likes and dislikes, and some quite radical suggestions were made as to how school might be changed.

I hope that studying the films will stimulate people to think about other systems of learning, and also to look more closely at the kind of education they have received, how it might be different, and what kind of system of learning they might construct for their children in the future – or do we need to construct systems at all? Imagination is free, and we all have that freedom to speculate about how people should learn and what they should learn about.

David Leland
January 1985

Useful addresses

Education Otherwise,
25 Common Lane,
Hemingford Abbots,
Cambs. PE18 9AN

Growing Without Schooling,
308 Boylston Street,
Boston,
Mass. 02116,
U.S.A.

Teach Your Own by John Holt, available from:
Lighthouse Books,
27a Sydney Street,
Brightlingsea,
Essex.

Flying into the Wind was first transmitted on ITV in Britain on 26 June 1983. Given below are the credits and cast for this Central production.

Credits

Production Manager	Donald Toms
1st Assistant Director	Guy Travers
Location Managers	Joanna Gollins, Paul Shersby
Continuity	Ene Watts
Production Assistant	Monica Rogers
2nd Assistant Directors	Roy Stevens, Chris Thompson
Camera Operator	Stephen Alcorn
Camera Assistants	Henry Marcuzzi, Adam Walton
Grip	Peter Hall
Gaffer	Ronnie Rampton
Boom Operator	Tony Bell
Sound Assistant	Clive Osborne
Dubbing Editor	Martin Evans
Editing Assistants	Cilla Beirne, Peter Bond
Make-up	Mary Hillman
Hairdresser	Joan Carpenter
Wardrobe	Daryl Bristow
Property Master	Bobby Hedges
Construction Charge Hand	John New
Accounts Assistant	Joan Murphy
Assistant Art Director	Celia Barnett
Costumes	Monica Howe
Production Executive	Sue Wall
Casting Director	Sheila Trezise
Sound Mixer	Tony Jackson
Dubbing Mixer	Trevor Pyke
Music by	Ronnie Leahy
Editor	Neil Thomson
Art Director	Jamie Leonard
Photographed by	Clive Tickner
Associate Producer	Patrick Cassavetti
Written by	David Leland
Producer	Margaret Matheson
Directed by	Edward Bennett

Cast

Judge Wood	Graham Crowden
Barry Wyatt	Derrick O'Connor
Sally Wyatt	Rynagh O'Grady
Michael	Adrian Wagstaff
Young Laura	Prudence Oliver
Mr Healey	Martin Duncan
Mr Spencer	Tim Preece
Miss Walker	Maggie Ford
Mr Harper	Tim Wylton
The Tramp	Alex McCrindle
Laura	Sallyanne Law
Mrs Grigsby	Lee Hudson
Doctor	Christopher Hancock
Karen Miles	Joanna Phillips-Lane
Mr Wiles	Arthur Whybrow
Nurse	Catherine Owen
Police Sergeant	Frank Mills
1st Teacher	Richard Albrecht
2nd Teacher	Helen Price
Mrs Lever	Phyllis Hickson
1st Policeman	Ben Robertson
2nd Policeman	Michael Simkins
Baby Michael	Rupert Thompson

Note on the text: The text which follows differs from the broadcast version of the film in a number of minor ways. A list of the changes is given in the appendix.

Flying into the Wind

Part One

| 1 | **Exterior. School. Day.** | 1 |

St Andrew's, a primary school situated in a working-class
district of Coventry. Built just after the turn of the century,
the building is typical of the period.

Caption: 1969

| 2 | **Interior. School. Day.** | 2 |

Camera moves through the school: empty corridors, coats
and hats, and a cloakroom. A piano with children singing can
be heard in the background.

| 3 | **Interior. Classroom. Day.** | 3 |

A first year junior class: the children are sitting at tables
reading their work books. As usual, in a class with children
of good reading ability, there is quite a wide selection of
books. The essential criteria of choice would be that the
books are, first, suitable to the comprehension of the
children; and, second, that they might also relate to various
work projects.

The teacher, KAREN MILES, mid/late twenties, is sitting at her
table listening to the children read passages from different
books. Each child comes up to the teacher's table and reads
quietly to the teacher, not to the class. A BOY of seven is
reading from the Narnia books.

The sound of this activity is somewhat muted, in the background.

We move through the classroom until we focus on LAURA WYATT. LAURA is seven, thin and fair. She has two books on her table: *Bangers and Mash*, a basic reading project book, and she is holding a large picture encyclopaedia. As she stares at the book, she intermittently moves her lips as if mouthing the words in the book to herself. Then she looks up and round at the class to see if any person is watching her.

4	**Exterior. Playground/Street. Day.**	4

The primary school playground. Noise of heavy traffic and the same classroom activities. The playground is empty.

Unseen by people in the classroom, LAURA WYATT walks alone out of an exterior door, across the expanse of tarmac of the empty playground towards the school gate.

5	**Exterior. Playground. Day.**	5

KAREN MILES, the teacher, is standing in the playground. She stands for some few seconds, motionless, slightly confused. She turns and walks back into the school.

> KAREN MILES
> . . . Laura . . . ?

6	**Exterior. Street. Day.**	6

A side street which leads down to a busy main road with heavy traffic.

LAURA walks out of the school gateway and walks down the side street towards the main road. She follows the high brick school wall down to the corner where she disappears from view.

7   Interior. House. Day.   7

The hallway of a small terraced house in Coventry. SALLY
WYATT slams down the telephone receiver. Total panic.

SALLY WYATT (30) is in the advanced stages of pregnancy.
She has been washing her hair; it has been combed through
but it is still wet. She is wearing a dress but no shoes.

She starts to run up the stairs. She turns before she reaches
the top and runs back down again. She goes into the living
room.

> SALLY WYATT
> (to herself)
> Oh, Christ, no . . . please . . . no.

A frantic search for her shoes. She finds them in the sitting
room. She hurries out of the sitting room, and quickly down
the hall to the front door. She is halfway out of the doorway
when she changes her mind. She comes back into the hall
and makes a grab for the telephone.

8   Int. Factory. Day.   8

The floor of a very large, long factory filled with machinery.

MR WILES, a supervisor, walks down the line until he reaches
BARRY WYATT (35).

People have to shout to be heard above the noise on the
factory floor. The dialogue is unheard:

> WILES
> . . . Barry.

> BARRY WYATT
> Mr Wiles.

> WILES
> Barry . . . can you come off a minute?

WYATT moves away from the machine.

> WILES
> Your wife just called.

> BARRY WYATT
> What's happened?

WILES moves WYATT away from his machine. He nods to the
FOREMAN who puts another WORKER into operation on
Wyatt's machine.

> WILES
> It's nothing serious. Your little girl, she got lost.

> BARRY WYATT
> What?!

> WILES
> I don't know the details. Just get off home as fast
> as you can.

They walk off down the line.

> WILES
> I'm sure it's nothing serious.

WYATT and WILES walk together for several yards and then
WYATT gradually increases his pace into a run.

9   Ext. Street. Day.   9

SALLY WYATT walks down a side street: a sense of unreality,
normal life is going on around her while she is in a state of
total crisis as she looks for her daughter.

10   Int./Ext. Street/School. Day.   10

The side street near the school. Not knowing where to go,
SALLY WYATT heads towards the school. A police Panda
patrol car is parked outside the entrance in the 'No Waiting'
area.

School has finished. The playground is empty. SALLY WYATT walks in through the gateway and into the deserted playground. She stands in the centre of the playground not knowing which way to go.

She makes for the classroom – in through the doorways and into Laura's classroom. Empty. She stands stranded in the empty classroom.

She is startled by a noise and turns to see a POLICEMAN standing in the doorway.

11   Ext. Street. Day.   11

The street of terraced houses where the Wyatts live.

BARRY WYATT drives into the street and overshoots the parking spot. He gets out of the car and dashes towards his house.

LAURA, his daughter, is sitting on the front door step.

>   BARRY WYATT
> Laura. What are you doing, love? Eh?
> Where's your mum?

He kneels beside her, hugs her, lifts her up.

>   BARRY WYATT
> Where've you been? Wha – you're all wet, love.

LAURA has wet herself.

>   BARRY WYATT
> What – oh, no. What's going on? What's all this?

LAURA begins to whimper. The police Panda patrol car pulls up outside the house. SALLY WYATT sees LAURA, gets out of the car.

>   BARRY WYATT
>   (angry)
> What the hell's going on?

| 12 | **Ext. Street. Night.** | 12 |

A shot of the exterior of the Wyatt's house at night. It has been raining. The street is quiet and empty.

| 13 | **Int. The Wyatt's house. Night.** | 13 |

Darkness. SALLY and BARRY WYATT are asleep in bed. LAURA can be heard crying.

> LAURA
> Mum . . . mum! Mummy . . . mum.

It is some moments before either of the parents stir. They have to pull themselves out of a dead sleep. LAURA continues to cry.

> BARRY WYATT
> Sal . . . Laura's crying.

> SALLY WYATT
> I know.

She is dragging herself out of bed. BARRY WYATT puts on the light.

> SALLY WYATT
> Coming, love, coming.

SALLY WYATT goes out onto the landing, turning on the landing light as she goes into Laura's bedroom. Signs of the new baby in Laura's room, a dismantled cot against the wall.

> SALLY WYATT
> What is it, Laura?

LAURA howls.

> SALLY WYATT
> What's the matter?

SALLY WYATT smells something. She pulls back the bed clothes. LAURA has fouled the bed.

> SALLY WYATT
> Oh, no, Laura. What have you done?

14   Int. Bathroom. Night.   14

LAURA is standing in the bath, naked, with a towel over her shoulders. She has her back towards her MOTHER who is washing her down.

WYATT moves into the bathroom so that he can look at and comfort LAURA.

> SALLY WYATT
> What have you done with the sheets?

> BARRY WYATT
> All taken care of, no problem.
> (to Laura)
> Eh, love? No problem.

LAURA does not react, she stares straight ahead at the wall.

> SALLY WYATT
> Never before, I don't understand it.

> BARRY WYATT
> It doesn't matter.

WYATT leaves the bathroom.

> SALLY WYATT
> (to Laura)
> Just turn round. Laura.
> (she turns her round)
> Come on, darling, almost finished.

LAURA does not react. She stares straight ahead, shaking.

SALLY WYATT is in the headmistress' office. MISS WALKER, the headmistress, is 40. She runs her school on established principles with an eye to new methods.

SALLY WYATT has been somewhat distressed by events, they have hit her at the wrong time causing ripples beneath the surface.

> WALKER
> She has reading and writing difficulties and her number work is poor.

> SALLY WYATT
> That was last year. I asked you about her last year.

> WALKER
> Yes.

> SALLY WYATT
> And you said she was very happy.

> WALKER
> She was in the infants, now she's in the juniors. That's when things usually come to the surface – any problems.

> SALLY WYATT
> Yes. Laura can't read or write, can she?

> WALKER
> It's not uncommon. I'm concerned, but I don't think you should be unduly distressed about it. There are usually two or three slow learners in every class.

> SALLY WYATT
> But why has it been ignored?

WALKER

It hasn't and it won't be. Now she's in the juniors, we concentrate much harder on the three Rs.

SALLY WYATT
(she almost cries)

Yes, but if she can't . . . can't she be put in a special class?

WALKER

I think we should consider that very carefully. Do you think she's disturbed about the new baby?

SALLY WYATT

. . . No.

WALKER

Was she in any trouble this morning?

SALLY WYATT

No. She was fine.

WALKER

I'll speak to Miss Miles at the end of the day, see how she's been. I think we should all get over yesterday before we do anything.

SALLY WYATT

Yes. She's not here today.

WALKER

Oh.

SALLY WYATT

I just, we just felt it better not to . . .

WALKER

I think it's important not to over-react. She mustn't feel she can get away with it.

The Wyatt's house.

In the kitchen
LAURA is cutting carrots on a board with a sharp knife.

BARRY WYATT, wearing an apron, is at the front door talking
to a neighbour, MRS GRIGSBY.

WYATT removes the apron as he walks back into the kitchen.

>   BARRY WYATT
> Laura. I've got to go over the road a minute. You
> stay here love.

>   LAURA
> I want to come with you.

>   BARRY WYATT
>   (going down the hall and out of the front
>   door)
> Stay there.

BARRY WYATT and MRS GRIGSBY cross over the road and go
into a house inhabited by Mrs Lever, an old lady in her mid-
eighties.

A few moments later, LAURA comes out of her front door,
crosses the road, and goes into Mrs Lever's house.

Mrs Lever's house. LAURA stands at the bottom of the stairs.
BARRY WYATT and MRS GRIGSBY stand at the top of the
stairs, outside the bathroom door with their backs to Laura.

MRS GRIGSBY talks to MRS LEVER who is in the bathroom –
she is unable to get out of the bath.

MRS GRIGSBY
Florrie, Florrie, you alright in there? I've got
Mr Wyatt, Florrie, we're coming in.

MRS LEVER
(from inside the bathroom)
No!

MRS GRIGSBY
I'm coming in, Florrie, just me, alright?

MRS GRIGSBY goes into the bathroom. BARRY WYATT waits
outside the door.

MRS LEVER
No . . . oh dear. No.

MRS GRIGSBY
Now don't be silly, Florrie. We've got to get you
out somehow.

MRS LEVER
I can manage.

MRS GRIGSBY
You'll slip and hurt yourself.

BARRY WYATT
Don't worry Mrs Lever, soon have you out of
there.

MRS LEVER
. . . No.

MRS GRIGSBY
It's alright, Florrie.

MRS LEVER
I'm not sure. I'm not sure at all.

BARRY WYATT goes into the bathroom. LAURA goes up to the
top of the stairs and, with great curiosity, watches what is
happening in the bathroom.

MRS GRIGSBY
Don't be silly, Florrie.

> BARRY WYATT
> Look, I'll just get you out of the tub, eh, and then I'll go, alright?

> MRS LEVER
> All this bother.

> BARRY WYATT
> No, no bother.

> MRS GRIGSBY
> Enough of this, Florrie. You ready Mr Wyatt?

> BARRY WYATT
> Yes, I'm ready. Up you come. That's it.

They are about to lift MRS LEVER from the bath when MRS GRIGSBY sees LAURA standing in the bathroom doorway. She slams the door shut with her foot.

Sound cuts to total silence. Close in on LAURA.

---

19   Int. Classroom. Day.   19

Noise of classroom activities in the background. Close in on LAURA who is sitting in the reading corner where the books are kept. She is holding the encyclopaedia picture book.

At the front of the class, MISS MILES is joined by a MAN (40) who is an educational psychologist. MISS MILES directs his attention towards LAURA.

---

20   Int. Bedroom. Night.   20

The Wyatt's bedroom. Darkness. SALLY WYATT wakes violently out of her sleep. LAURA is crying in the next room. A distressed cry.

> LAURA
> Mummy!

BARRY WYATT is driving LAURA to school. LAURA is sitting in the back seat. She is distraught, howling loud and strong. WYATT, angry and frustrated, is ready to shout and bully to get the child to school.

Laura's objections run right through Wyatt's dialogue.

> LAURA
> Please daddy, please take me home.

> BARRY WYATT
> You can't not go to school . . . bloody hell . . . Laura! Look, I don't care, you can scream your bloody guts out, I don't care, you're going!

> LAURA
> No. I don't want to go. Please dad. Please. I don't want to go to school. Take me home. Mum. Mummy!

> BARRY WYATT
> What's the matter with you? All the other kids go to school! They don't scream their heads off every bleedin' morning, do they?

> LAURA
> Take me home. Take me home. Take me home.

WYATT stops the car near the school.

> BARRY WYATT
> (tense)
> Look, I've got to go to work. Where do you think the money comes from? I'm late for work now, I'm late.

> LAURA
> Please, I want to go home daddy.

> BARRY WYATT
> (getting out of the door)
> I go to work. You go to school.

> LAURA
> No . . . no . . . I don't want to go. Please, please, no.

LAURA is getting quite hysterical. WYATT pulls her out of the back of the car. She continues to struggle and cry as WYATT carries her in through the school gateway.

---

22   **Ext. Playground. Day.**   **22**

WYATT carries LAURA in through the gateway. Lined up at the gateway is LAURA'S CLASS. They are about to go to the local pool for a swimming lesson.

> BARRY WYATT
> Don't worry . . . it's alright once you get inside there . . . just . . .

MISS WALKER, the headmistress, walks towards them from the school. WYATT stops, weakened in his resolve for the first time. He puts LAURA down, kneels in front of her.

> WALKER
> Mr Wyatt.

> BARRY WYATT
> I'm sorry, she's a bit upset. Look, come on, Laura.

> WALKER
> Come along, Laura. Give her to me, Mr Wyatt.

LAURA clings to her father. WYATT tries to prise her hands away.

> BARRY WYATT
> Come on, love.

> LAURA
> No.

BARRY WYATT
There's no need for all this.

LAURA
Please, daddy, please.

BARRY WYATT
Look Laura, I'm late for work.

LAURA continues howling, tears streaming down her face.

WALKER
It's alright, Mr Wyatt. Come on, Laura, come with
me. You can come into the classroom with me.
You needn't go swimming, alright?

BARRY WYATT
I didn't know there was swimming today.

WALKER
Laura.

BARRY WYATT
I don't have any of her stuff.

WALKER
It's alright. Laura! I'm not going to have it.
Enough of all this. Everybody's looking at you –
now come along!

LAURA clings to her father. WYATT shakes his head.

LAURA
No . . . no . . . no!

BARRY WYATT
I'm not so sure about this. Look at the state of her.

WALKER
If you weaken now, you'll pay the price later.

BARRY WYATT
(trying to quieten Laura)
It's OK. Thanks very much.

WYATT walks with LAURA towards the playground exit.

> WALKER
> If you don't get her in now, she'll never catch up,
> she'll never learn.

23   Ext. Street. Day.   23

Wyatt's car rolls slowly to a stop outside the family home.

WYATT sits, defeated and depressed. LAURA is in the back
seat, sad, having gained nothing from her victory.

> BARRY WYATT
> (unheard)
> Come on, love, it's not the end of the world.

From a house several doors down the street, MRS GRIGSBY
appears and, waving to WYATT, runs towards them as fast as
she can.

WYATT winds down the car window.

> MRS GRIGSBY
> You should be at work.

> BARRY WYATT
> Yeah . . . I know.

> MRS GRIGSBY
> They phoned you at work.

> BARRY WYATT
> . . . Who did?

> MRS GRIGSBY
> It's Sally, your wife, love, they've taken her in.

24   Int. Hospital Corridor. Day.   24

WYATT, holding LAURA's hand, moves quickly down the
corridor towards the maternity ward.

LAURA has to run to keep up with him.

> NURSE
> Mr Wyatt?

> BARRY WYATT
> Yeah, that's right.

> NURSE
> Your wife's in there.

> BARRY WYATT
> Is it alright if I take her in for a minute?

> NURSE
> . . . I'm sorry.

> BARRY WYATT
> I can go in?

> NURSE
> Of course.

> BARRY WYATT
> Laura, I'm just going in to see your mum, just for a
> minute. You stay there and wait.

WYATT goes into the delivery room. LAURA is left standing
outside staring at another closed door. The NURSE sits on a
bench.

> NURSE
> Laura. Laura, why don't you sit down? Daddy will
> be back in a minute. Would you like to come and
> sit down next to me?

LAURA does not move. The NURSE goes over to LAURA and
stands behind her.

> NURSE
> Do you want a little sister or a little brother?

LAURA does not react.

> NURSE
> (touching her on the shoulder)
Laura.

LAURA reacts, startled by the NURSE's touch.

> NURSE
> (taking Laura's hand)
> Here. Come and sit over here.

The NURSE takes LAURA to the bench where they both sit down and wait in silence.

WYATT comes out of the delivery room.

> BARRY WYATT
> (to the nurse)
> I'll go back and see. They said it'll be quick.

> NURSE
> Mr Wyatt, I'm sorry, but when you came in I didn't realize.

> BARRY WYATT
> (he does not understand)
> Realize? Realize what?

> NURSE
> . . . about your daughter. I didn't realize she's deaf.

WYATT looks at LAURA who is sitting alone on the bench.

25   Ext. Street. Day.   25

EDWARD HARPER (42), Education Welfare Officer, is knocking on the Wyatt's front door. After a couple of knocks, he takes a look through the letter box just as SALLY WYATT opens the front room window.

The hall and kitchen have been redecorated, chairs are piled in the hall and there's a step-ladder.

> HARPER
> Ah – yes. Mrs Wyatt. Harper. Education Welfare
> Officer. I sent you a note.

> SALLY WYATT
> Yes. You'd better come in. It would be easier this
> way.

HARPER climbs in through the front room window. SALLY
WYATT closes the window behind him.

26   Int. Kitchen/Hall. Day.   26

SALLY WYATT has cleared a space on the table and is making
a stew.

HARPER has a file in which he has details of the WYATT's
case.

> HARPER
> And what else did the doctor say?

> SALLY WYATT
> They could find nothing wrong with her – we took
> her to more than one.

> HARPER
> Is she still deaf?

> SALLY WYATT
> No, she's not.

> HARPER
> If the child is fit and well she should be in school.

> SALLY WYATT
> She could go deaf again.

LAURA carries a kitchen chair from the hall into the kitchen.

> SALLY WYATT
> There's no need to do that, Laura.

HARPER
This is Laura. Hello, Laura.

LAURA
Hello.

SALLY WYATT
(to Harper)
Please use that, please sit down –

SALLY WYATT goes back to cutting the meat. LAURA
continues to ferry chairs from the hall into the kitchen.

HARPER
Laura has been away from school for one and
three-quarter terms now.

SALLY WYATT
Yes.

HARPER
Well, she's got difficulties, we must sort them out.

SALLY WYATT
She doesn't.

HARPER
Well, she does have certain learning disabilities,
we do know that, Mrs Wyatt, and so do you.

SALLY WYATT
Sombody else used that term. What does it mean?

HARPER
Compared with other children, lack of ability to
grasp certain rudimentary functions.

SALLY WYATT
You mean she's dim.

HARPER
That's not the point, and you know that.

SALLY WYATT
Do you think she's retarded?

> HARPER
> I don't know. Mrs Wyatt, the point is that Laura
> can get worse through neglect. If you carry on like
> this you could have a severely maladjusted child
> on your hands. She needs help.

> SALLY WYATT
> You think she's maladjusted?

> HARPER
> Mrs Wyatt, I've told you, I don't know.

LAURA brings in another chair.

> HARPER
> We need more information.

HARPER pauses until LAURA is out of the room. LAURA
knows who they are talking about.

> HARPER
> We'd like her to see the educational psychologist
> again.

> SALLY WYATT
> Again?

> HARPER
> Yes. She's already been seen by a psychologist at
> the school. Did you not know that?

> SALLY WYATT
> No. I didn't.

In the hall
LAURA is taking the carrycot out of the living room and
placing it on the metal frame and wheels standing near the
door.

> HARPER
> The point is, as long as Laura is not in school she's
> not learning anything, is she? Now, the child has
> to be pointed in the right direction.

In the kitchen

SALLY WYATT
I don't think there is anything wrong with Laura.

HARPER
Good. Then she should be in school.

SALLY WYATT
I don't think there is anything wrong with Laura except school.

HARPER
Ah! I see – everything and everybody is wrong except my child!

SALLY WYATT
Mr Harper, I don't believe in force and I have no intention of forcing Laura into something that does her harm, into something she hates. She's made that perfectly clear and I trust Laura, Mr Harper, I trust her.

She hears Laura on the stairs and she hears the baby.

SALLY WYATT
Excuse me.

She goes into the hall. HARPER watches from the kitchen door.

LAURA is coming down the steep staircase with the baby, MICHAEL, in her arms. MICHAEL is now 3–4 months old.

LAURA's descent is precarious and HARPER is somewhat alarmed.

SALLY WYATT
What are you doing, love?

LAURA
I'm taking Michael for a walk.

HARPER
Mind those stairs . . .

LAURA has never done this before. SALLY WYATT is stunned, but tries not to show it. LAURA puts MICHAEL in the carrycot.

> LAURA
> I won't be long.

> SALLY WYATT
> I'll help you out with the pram.

> LAURA
> I'll do it.

LAURA pulls the pram back down the hall so that she can then open the front door.

SALLY WYATT puts her hand onto the pram. She looks down at MICHAEL to make sure he's tucked in properly.

LAURA pushes the pram through the front doorway and into the street: a bumpy, difficult manoeuvre.

> SALLY WYATT
> See you later.

She closes the front door, cutting off her view of LAURA and the pram, and turns towards HARPER.

> HARPER
> Mrs Wyatt . . . has she not done that before?

> SALLY WYATT
> No, never.

> HARPER
> Is that wise?

She walks past MR HARPER into the kitchen and continues to cut the meat, but her mind is with LAURA and MICHAEL.

> HARPER
> Look, Mrs Wyatt, you have to send your child to school, that's the law.

SALLY WYATT
Laura doesn't want to go to school.

HARPER
If you provoke the authorities, they'll have to take action.

SALLY WYATT
I'm not going to provoke anybody.

HARPER
Such decisions cannot be taken on the whim of the child. You are responsible. The child has no such right. You can't just leave her out of school.

SALLY WYATT
What if we do?

HARPER
The authority could not allow it. We also have responsibilities, we have the right to intervene on behalf of the child.

SALLY WYATT
What would happen?

HARPER
If you didn't send her?

SALLY WYATT
Yes.

HARPER
Well, you will be served with a school attendance order instructing you to send your child to school.

SALLY WYATT
If not?

HARPER
Well, you'll be summonsed.

SALLY WYATT
Then what – if we still don't send her to school?

HARPER
Let's hope it doesn't get that far.

SALLY WYATT
What if it does come to that?

HARPER
Your child could be taken away. She could be put
into care.

27   Ext. Street. Day.   27

LAURA and MICHAEL in his pram. The end of the road lets
out onto waste ground; beyond that, a council estate.

On the waste ground: TWO BOYS, truants, are throwing
bricks at each other. A bit further off, THREE VAGRANTS are
squatting near a fire made from old rubbish boxes.

28   Int. Courtroom. Day.   28

1980.

This is a Court of Appeal held in Crown Court.

JUDGE WOOD sits in a large, red chair with the Queen's crest
imprinted on its back. To his left, a MALE MAGISTRATE in his
mid-fifties. To his right, a FEMALE MAGISTRATE in her early
forties.

MR HEALEY, a barrister in his thirties, appears for the Local
Education Authority. MR SPENCER, in his early forties,
appears for the appellants, the Wyatts.

Also present in the court are SOLICITORS, REPRESENTATIVES
of the L.E.A., EXPERT WITNESSES for both sides, a FEMALE
COURT USHER, and there is a MALE CLERK of the court who
sports a large, shaggy beard.

There is a public gallery – empty. And there is one lone
REPORTER on the press bench.

BARRY WYATT is seated near his solicitor and SALLY WYATT is in the witness box.

Next to BARRY WYATT is a young woman of eighteen. She is wearing a dress. This is LAURA.

JUDGE WOOD reads from Halsbury.

> JUDGE WOOD
> 'It shall be the duty of the parent of every child of compulsory school age to cause him to receive efficient full-time education suitable to his age, ability and aptitude, either by regular attendance at school or otherwise.'

> SPENCER
> Yes, Your Honour. The law expressly preserves the freedom for parents not to send their children to school.

> JUDGE WOOD
> 'or otherwise'.

> SPENCER
> Yes, Your Honour.

> JUDGE WOOD
> But it is the local authority's responsibility to see that the children receive *'efficient full-time education'*, is it not?

> SPENCER
> If the local authority is not satisfied the children are receiving an efficient education they serve a school attendance order on the parents – as we see has happended to this family.

> JUDGE WOOD
> On numerous occasions.

> SPENCER
> The attendance order merely requires the parents to send their child to school. But, in the last resort,

it is for the court, this court, to decide as to the *suitability* of the child's education, *not* the local authority.

JUDGE WOOD

Yes.

SPENCER

Mrs Wyatt, you've been in court on a number of occasions for failing to send your children, Laura and Michael, to school. You pleaded guilty on those occasions.

SALLY WYATT

Yes. Guilty to not complying with the school attendance orders. But we are not guilty of failing to provide our children with a proper education.

JUDGE WOOD

That is a matter of opinion, not of fact, Mrs Wyatt. That is the nature of your appeal. If you are providing your child with an 'efficient full-time education suitable to his age, ability and aptitude', as laid down in the Education Act, then this appeal against your conviction in the Magistrate's Court will be granted – and the education authorities will no longer be obliged to serve orders on you to send your child to school.

SPENCER

Precisely, Your Honour. Mrs Wyatt, at the time you first took Laura out of school she was having great difficulty with her reading and writing.

SALLY WYATT

She could not read at all.

SPENCER

Can she read now?

SALLY WYATT

She can, but only to herself.

41

SPENCER
How long has she been reading?

SALLY WYATT
For two years, since she was sixteen – she's now
eighteen.

SPENCER
And Michael?

SALLY WYATT
He cannot read at all.

JUDGE WOOD
How old is Michael?

SALLY WYATT
Eleven.

JUDGE WOOD
He is eleven and cannot read at all.

SALLY WYATT
That is correct.

---

29   Ext. Gravel Pit. Day.   29

At the end of a rough track leading from the Wyatt's home,
there is a gravel pit.

It is an old, pre-war excavation, dug in the days when
contractors were not obliged to restore the landscape to its
natural contours after removing the sand and gravel. Mud
and dirt removed to get at the gravel were left in mounds
around the pit.

On one side, there is open, clear water. On the other, a mass
of reeds and bullrushes. Away to the right, there is a wooden
catwalk, rotten and covered in green moss.

MICHAEL WYATT is lying on his stomach on the catwalk
looking over the edge into the water.

Part Two

Summer.

The flat, black terrain of the Lincolnshire countryside.

Standing well back from a 'B' road is the Wyatt's home.
Apart from the small, renovated house, there are numerous
outbuildings constructed from slatted wood and corrugated
tin.

There are two dismembered hulks of Morris Minor cars used
as a source for spare parts to construct one functional car.

There is also a clapped-out commercial van which, when
started, sounds as if it's at death's door and lets out volumes
of black smoke.

The homestead is a failed small-holding, bleak and
unyielding.

LAURA cycles along the track which leads to the house. It has
been raining. SALLY WYATT is at the front door.

> LAURA
> Hello, mum.

> SALLY WYATT
> Hello, Laura.

> SPENCER
> You have told us how Laura went deaf.

> SALLY WYATT
> Yes. At school, she was required to read and
> write. Laura understood what was required but
> could not do it.

SPENCER
Because of dyslexia.

SALLY WYATT
That's right.

SPENCER
How did you discover Laura was dyslexic?

SALLY WYATT
On the advice of a friend, we approached a
Dr Powell and she diagnosed dyslexia.

SPENCER
Your Honour, Dr Margaret Powell is a
psychologist working at the University of East
Anglia and I would like to submit as evidence the
report she made at that time.

JUDGE WOOD
Any objections, Mr Healey?

HEALEY
No, Your Honour.

JUDGE WOOD
Do you want us to read this now, Mr Spencer?

SPENCER
With respect, Your Honour, I do not consider that
to be necessary. I would only ask the court to note
that what was diagnosed in Laura was not in any
sense a disability. Essentially, dyslexia is a
difference in the capacity of ease with which the
child acquires certain skills, particularly reading
and writing. It will be evident that for children
who are different in this way the school system
can be very difficult. The child becomes caught up
in a race to catch up with the 'normal' or 'bright'
child. Because of the high emphasis put on
academic learning, they will likely be regarded as
retarded or backward when, in fact, they are not.

JUDGE WOOD
Does this report refer to Michael, Mr Spencer?

SPENCER
No, Your Honour.

JUDGE WOOD
Laura's educational history is only of interest to
this court in as much as it informs us of the
educational approach to Michael. He is the only
one of school age.

SPENCER
Precisely, that is correct, Your Honour.

JUDGE WOOD
Is Michael dyslexic?

SALLY WYATT
We believe he is, yes.

JUDGE WOOD
Has Michael been diagnosed as dyslexic by
Dr Powell or any other expert?

SALLY WYATT
No, Your Honour. He has never been tested or
assessed by any expert.

JUDGE WOOD
And yet you believe him to be dyslexic.

SALLY WYATT
Yes.

JUDGE WOOD
Why have you not confirmed this?

SALLY WYATT
Because it would not alter our approach to his
education.

JUDGE WOOD
I beg your pardon?

SALLY WYATT
Because it would not alter our approach to his
education.

32   Int. Workshop. Day.   32

Among the outbuildings there is an old workshop. It is quite
a large building.

In the workshop, BARRY WYATT and MICHAEL are building a
boat. They are constructing a very simple pram dinghy.

The Wyatts are not expert boat builders and do not use ideal
methods or materials. They are learning as they go along,
with a plan to guide their work.

As the two people work together, it is very clear that
MICHAEL is skilled at using the various machines.

33   Int. Courtroom. Day.   33

SPENCER
Michael cannot read and write.

SALLY WYATT
No.

SPENCER
Does that concern you?

SALLY WYATT
I believe it is important he learns to read and
write, yes, but I don't believe it's for me to impose
on him how or when he should do this. I believe
he will learn in his own time.

SPENCER
What are you doing to teach him to read?

SALLY WYATT
It is his need to learn to read and write that

matters the most. My job is to watch and see what sparks his interest and to follow that, provide for that – even it it does not appear to make sense at first.

SPENCER
What do you mean by 'follow'?

SALLY WYATT
I mean the parents' part is to follow the needs of the child, to provide for that the best way we can – either at home or in the work that we do. Or we go to an outside source – books, travel to see people and places, anything. It takes a lot of effort, but it can be very rewarding. There are a lot of people out there with information to give and skills to teach, retired people for example. Once you ask, people can be very generous.

JUDGE WOOD
Yes, Mrs Wyatt, but the fact is Michael still cannot read.

SALLY WYATT
No.

JUDGE WOOD
So all that does not solve the problem.

SALLY WYATT
I do not see it as a problem, Your Honour.

JUDGE WOOD
If Michael is dyslexic and cannot read, then surely that is a problem.

SALLY WYATT
When Laura was first diagnosed as dyslexic I saw it as a terrible problem, but I don't think like that now.

JUDGE WOOD
We are discussing Michael.

SALLY WYATT

I do not think the illiterate really have a problem, that is the point I am making, Your Honour. I think we are the problem – society that is – because we insist on making them a problem. People who can't write are inferior, that's the attitude. We have the idea that if you cannot read and write you cannot do anything else. One sees the same attitude towards the physically disabled. If you allow people the freedom to talk for themselves then you hear a different story.

| 34 | **Ext. Lincolnshire. Day.** | 34 |

The flat Lincolnshire landscape stretches into miles.

In the distance, barely visible, a FIGURE walks along the track towards the Wyatt's house.

Something slightly ominous about this image.

| 35 | **Int./Ext. Workshop/Yard. Day.** | 35 |

The workshop is well equipped. There is a full range of hand carpentry tools and also tools for plumbing, a mortice and tenon cutter, a router, a jig saw, a circular saw, a drill on a stand, etc. A lot of the equipment, including the tools, is quite old. They have shopped around and bought stuff from local country auctions.

The frame of the boat is now well advanced. BARRY WYATT is welding, MICHAEL is fixing a screw to the frame of the boat.

MICHAEL has long been able to use tools and machinery which would usually be considered dangerous for an eleven-year-old boy. He has developed a skill and confidence beyond what might be considered normal for a boy of his age.

Suddenly MICHAEL's concentration is broken and he looks sharply up towards the workshop door.

>   MICHAEL
> Dad.

BARRY WYATT turns off the welder and, directed by MICHAEL, looks towards the door.

Standing in the doorway, watching BARRY and MICHAEL, is a man in his mid-sixties. He is a TRAMP.

>   TRAMP
> Good afternoon.

>   BARRY WYATT
> Hello.

>   TRAMP
> Could you fill me drum, give me a bite to eat, boss?

>   BARRY WYATT
> Yeah. Yeah, sure, hang on a minute.

BARRY WYATT walks out of the garage and towards the house. MICHAEL stares at the TRAMP. The TRAMP looks back in MICHAEL's direction and watches him for some moments. Hold on MICHAEL's view of the TRAMP.

>   TRAMP
>   (pointing to himself)
> Tired.

36   Int. Courtroom. Day.   36

HEALEY cross-examines SALLY WYATT. HEALEY has an irritating habit, common among barristers, of not appearing to listen to the answers to the questions he has just asked.

>   HEALEY
> How is your approach different to the approach of a school?

SALLY WYATT

First, we concentrate on what they can do, rather than what they cannot do. We follow the needs of the child.

HEALEY

I'm not at all sure what you mean by that, Mrs Wyatt: how exactly does one do that – 'follow the needs of the child'?

SALLY WYATT

I've already explained. Our society isn't in the habit of following the needs of the child, that's why we give them things like concrete playgrounds; they fit the needs of the adult.

HEALEY

Yes, but I still have no clear picture of how your approach of 'following the child' differs from that of the average school.

SALLY WYATT

Well, we don't have a curriculum for a start, we don't have a set routine, we don't sit down and do lessons. Whereas a school would concentrate on what the child finds difficult, we concentrate on what they enjoy doing; we don't set standards, we don't give them so many marks out of ten.

HEALEY

Who decides on what activity is to be followed?

SALLY WYATT

They do. They must decide for themselves.

HEALEY

They are allowed to follow whatever activity they choose.

SALLY WYATT

Yes.

HEALEY

For as long as they like?

SALLY WYATT

Yes.

HEALEY

And no one ever corrects them, even if they've made the wrong decision.

SALLY WYATT

The best way to discover that is through experience, not by being told not to do something. The essence of learning is experience. Children are very quick to abandon what does not interest them.

HEALEY

Don't you feel that sometimes they must be made to face a difficult task in order to learn?

SALLY WYATT

No, never. They must set their own standards.

HEALEY

So, in your system – if it is a system – children do not have to measure up to any objective standards in what they are doing. If they set out to do a task, they are free to abandon it if they wish to, or to continue it as long as they like and nobody will stop, correct or guide them in any way – is that correct?

SALLY WYATT

We don't tell our children what to do or how to do it; they must take their own decisions.

HEALEY

Let us take an example. Suppose Michael wanted to go fishing all day – some children will go fishing all day and every day, if given the chance – what would you do?

SALLY WYATT

We don't make the kind of distinctions between work and play which are behind the question.

HEALEY

That is a very idealistic and somewhat patronizing answer to a very simple question. If Michael wanted to go out fishing every day, what would you do?

SALLY WYATT

It just doesn't happen, not like that. It's difficult . . . you see, I think it's difficult for us to understand this. We have been brought up with the feeling that work takes one away from the things one really enjoys. Why should it be like this? It's not like that for them.

JUDGE WOOD

Mrs Wyatt, what you are really being asked is, as I understand it, is there anyone who can tell Michael if he is right or not? Do you follow?

SALLY WYATT

They are self-assessing, Your Honour. They decide how well they are doing. It is success or failure on their own terms, nobody else's. We say to our children, 'only you have the answers to your own lives'. That has nothing to do with dyslexia. It's not a soft approach, it's very tough. The world is changing quickly and violently – they must have the ability to control their own lives and create their own standards. It takes time and effort to create an environment where children can find out, where they can discover themselves. Just as it has taken time and effort to deprive them of that privilege and to construct an educational system where they are given the idea that parents, teachers, somebody, anybody other than themselves, has got all the answers and that their part in that is simply to do as they're told, to sit back and wait for the information to be vended to them.

                    HEALEY
And yet Michael is eleven and cannot read.

                    SALLY WYATT
Not yet.

---

37   **Ext. Yard. Day.**   **37**

Late afternoon.

MICHAEL stands before the TRAMP. The tramp's drum is full
of tea. He has two hefty sandwiches, a couple of pickled
onions and a mug of tea.

The TRAMP talks and eats.

> TRAMP
> This is my last big skipper and then back to Bristol.
> I got a caravan rent free, night-watchman for a
> truck firm, but it's still rough. I've got a sense of
> direction. I like the tracks, away from the roads,
> across the fields. I've been to Canada, freighting,
> riding the big locomotives. Walking. Norman
> Wells, Fort Good Hope, Fort Independent, Fort
> Rigley, Fort Resolution, the Great Slave Lake,
> Yellow Knife – on the Slave – and over the top to
> Great Bear and into the Arctic Circle. There were
> Eskimos and Ejibu Indians. I came back just before
> the war. I lived in a hut in Mapes Wood for
> twenty-nine years and four months. Then the
> Social Security wanted to help. Rehabilitation. So I
> left. If you live a tough life you have to live it till
> you're dead. Get soft, you won't last long.

---

38   **Ext. Yard. Day.**   **38**

MICHAEL stands watching the TRAMP walk off down a rough
cart track which leads away from the road into the open
countryside.

MICHAEL walks back to where his FATHER is finishing off the day's work on the boat.

HEALEY

Is there any difference then, so far as you are concerned, between life for your children and education?

SALLY WYATT

No, life is education. All life. For most people, education has become a preparation for work, then life becomes work. We do not believe that is education.

HEALEY

As far as you are concerned, every experience they have from the moment they wake up until they go to sleep is part of their education.

SALLY WYATT

There are no set hours, if that's what you mean. Yes, it's a continuous education. It isn't a matter of what facts you know – more a matter of finding and getting the facts you need, learning how to use what you've got in a constantly changing situation. That's not pie in the sky, that's a tough assignment. Children with heads stuffed full of facts and figures do not interest me. The quest for ideas, that is what we are trying to achieve.

HEALEY

If, for example, Michael wrote a story or a letter – if he could write – would you correct it?

SALLY WYATT

If he asked me to correct it, yes.

HEALEY

If not, you would leave it uncorrected.

SALLY WYATT

Yes.

HEALEY

You would allow him to send the letter uncorrected.

SALLY WYATT

Yes, of course. What is important is the child's sense of achievement, not the quality of the spelling or punctuation.

HEALEY

And yet Michael is eleven and still cannot read, and Laura did not learn to read until she was sixteen.

SALLY WYATT

That is correct.

HEALEY

Do you not think she might have learned to read much earlier if she had gone to school in the usual way?

SALLY WYATT

That's not important. You keep looking for a standard. You must be here at such and such a time. That's what happens in schools. It's a fiercely competitive attitude and it sets people against each other right from the start.

HEALEY

Yes, but what you are describing to me as an alternative, Mrs Wyatt, is nothing more than a creative form of truancy. By adopting your policy of 'the children will learn to read when they want to learn to read', you are neglecting – more than that – you are abandoning the learning potential of your children to read and write. You have made no active attempts to rectify Michael's basic lack of skill in this area. By denying him the facilities of a

HEALEY *(continued)*
full-time education, as the law requires, you are
failing to cause your son to receive education
'suitable to his age, ability and aptitude'. How can
this kind of negligence be categorized as efficient
education?

40   Ext. Gravel Pit. Day.   40

At the end of the rough track is the gravel pit.

The van is reversed to within a few yards of the water's edge.
BARRY WYATT and MICHAEL get out of the van.

BARRY WYATT
Better not get too close. We'll never get out. It's
dead soft here.

They open the back of the van.

MICHAEL
Shall I get in and push?

BARRY WYATT
No, we can lug it out from here.

They haul the boat out of the back of the van and begin to
drag it to the water's edge.

41   Int. Courtroom. Day.   41

HEALEY
Do you not think the knowledge and experience of
adults, you in particular, has anything to offer
your children by guiding them?

SALLY WYATT
By guiding them, no.

HEALEY
Then how is the child to learn?

SALLY WYATT

When you push people into doing things, you drive them away from their own true interests –

HEALEY

I was talking of guidance –

SALLY WYATT

I think it's the same thing – 'guidance', 'control', 'structure' – to me it's all the same thing. You assume that children will not learn anything useful unless we, the adults, guide them and show them how.

HEALEY

Most children will learn very little if left to their own devices.

SALLY WYATT

It depends on the quality of the environment we provide for them. We must look to ourselves.

HEALEY

But I repeat, Mrs Wyatt, how is the child to learn?

SALLY WYATT

You speak about learning as if it was the last thing children wanted to do.

HEALEY

Mrs Wyatt, you are doing absolutely nothing to cope with the complex difficulties Michael has with reading and writing.

SALLY WYATT

We have changed our whole lives. We have presented long lists and schedules to the court as evidence of our efforts to create a learning environment. There is a limit to what I can tell you: if you want to know more, the best way is to see for yourself.

JUDGE WOOD
That is not out of the question. The court may
decide to do that, Mrs Wyatt. Isn't this the point –
aren't a lot of children a bit lazy? If you get
someone a bit lazy you may find that he does not
want to learn to read. Does he not then need a
little external stimulation in the form of a prod?

42	**Ext. Gravel Pit. Day.**	42

The boat has been launched. BARRY WYATT sits in the centre
of the boat, and is gently rowing the boat across the water.
MICHAEL sits in the stern, facing his father.

MICHAEL
Roach . . . Dace . . .

BARRY WYATT
Rudd.

MICHAEL
Rudd. Carp. Perch.

BARRY WYATT
Perch.

MICHAEL
Minnows – pike!

BARRY WYATT
Mackerel.

MICHAEL
No.

BARRY WYATT
Yes – skate, haddock, cod and chips.

An underwater view of the gravel pit. The water is very clear and deep.

MICHAEL is leaning over the back of the boat looking into the water through a small glass-bottomed viewing box.

> MICHAEL
> It's really deep.

> BARRY WYATT
> Yes. What can you see?

> MICHAEL
> Loads of weeds, all waving. It's really clear, you can see right down to the bottom.

> BARRY WYATT
> What else?

> MICHAEL
> Nothing. Just water. How deep is it?

> BARRY WYATT
> Thirty feet.

> MICHAEL
> That's deep.

> BARRY WYATT
> That's why you should be wearing a life jacket.

> MICHAEL
> I can swim.

> BARRY WYATT
> What, with your boots and clothes on?

> MICHAEL
> How do you know it's thirty feet?

> BARRY WYATT
> I don't exactly, could be more. You can always measure.

                    MICHAEL
How?

                    BARRY WYATT
Six foot rule – jump in and keep going till you hit
the bottom. Go in any further over there and
you'll go arse over tit, mate.

                    MICHAEL
You can see everything, dad.

Beneath the water, from beneath the boat, a face appears.

On the surface, in the boat

                    MICHAEL
I saw a face.

44   Ext. Gravel Pit. Day.   44

Long shot as the boat takes a slow circuitous route round the
gravel pit to the spot where Michael has seen the face under
the water.

BARRY WYATT clambers to the stern of the boat, MICHAEL
sits in the centre of the boat.

BARRY WYATT leans over the stern and looks down into the
water through the viewing box.

Beneath the water
A thirty-foot drop to the bottom of the pit. Clear water.
Nothing.

MICHAEL rows the boat, taking it on a few feet.

Beneath the water
First the boots. Then the trousers. Overcoat billowing, full of
water. The face. BARRY WYATT is stunned.

In the boat
                    MICHAEL
It's the man, isn't it? The man who came to the
house. The man who had the sandwiches.

WYATT has not recognized the man. He realizes that Michael is correct.

BARRY WYATT
. . . Yeah.

MICHAEL watches his father.

MICHAEL
You frightened, dad?

BARRY WYATT
No . . . Yeah, well, a bit, yeah.

BARRY WYATT becomes aware that MICHAEL is studying him quite closely and that his own reaction to the dead man beneath the water is of considerable importance to his son. MICHAEL's first reaction is one of curiosity.

BARRY WYATT
I wonder how he got in there, eh?

MICHAEL
Is he dead?

BARRY WYATT
Yeah, I should think so, mate. Dead as mutton.

They change places in the boat again. BARRY WYATT takes up the oars and begins to row for the shore.

MICHAEL
Are we going home, dad?

BARRY WYATT
We got to tell somebody – can't leave him down there can we? Police, let them deal with it.

MICHAEL looks back to where they sighted the body. He is still curious.

MICHAEL
Will he stay where he is, or will he move? Can't see him any more.

The boat hits shore; BARRY WYATT scrambles out. He holds out his hand for MICHAEL.

> MICHAEL
> How will they get him out, dad?

> BARRY WYATT
> Oh, they got all the right gear to get him out.

> MICHAEL
> What do they do?

> BARRY WYATT
> Tell the truth, mate, I don't really know. Don't worry about it, they'll get him out alright.

> MICHAEL
> Can we watch?

45   Int. Courtroom. Day.   45
───

> SALLY WYATT
> Your Honour, I believe that laziness is what happens when children have their initiative taken away from them. We give children the idea that we, the adults, have all the answers and their part is simply to do as they're told and learn. That's what happens in schools. That's the system, and unless you have the money there are no other alternatives other than to take your children out of school.

> HEALEY
> You don't particularly like the state system, do you, Mrs Wyatt?

> SALLY WYATT
> Since taking my children out of school, I've learned an awful lot about it.

> HEALEY
> You have very little time for it.

SALLY WYATT

It's certainly not beyond criticism, but I've only given you my views so that you might understand our approach more clearly.

HEALEY

If left to his own devices, Michael might be thirty or forty before he learns to read. Or he may not learn to read at all.

SALLY WYATT

Possibly, in which case he will join the ranks of the two million illiterate adults we already have in this country.

HEALEY

Let us confine ourselves to Michael.

SALLY WYATT

We have considered the possibility. He may not learn to read or write. If so, it means he must have more confidence than the average person to be able to stand up and say, 'I cannot read'.

HEALEY

But all that may not be necessary, Mrs Wyatt, when a little bit of guidance and control could make all the difference.

SALLY WYATT

It's a matter of trust. If a child is one hundred per cent absorbed in what he or she is doing, I cannot see that I would be the one to stop them and point them in another direction.

HEALEY

Surely, even in an alternative education system, would it not be both desirable and essential for the child, particularly a dyslexic child, to receive some kind of guidance from the adult?

SALLY WYATT

But to do that we presume that the adult knows
best. 'Trust us, do what we, the adults, tell you
and your future will be secure.' How many
children have swallowed that only to become
bitter and disillusioned? Why do we never
consider unconditioning the adult mind and not
conditioning the child?

46   Ext. Gravel Pit. Day.   46

Three vehicles are parked at the end of the track near the
gravel pit: a police van, a police car, and the undertaker's
black Ford Cortina hearse.

TWO POLICEMEN are searching round the edge of the pit
near the catwalk.

FROGMEN are diving from a dinghy in the centre of the pit.

A police SERGEANT is standing at the water's edge watching
the action. MICHAEL is just behind him. BARRY WYATT and
the DOCTOR are looking on.

Over on the catwalk, the TWO POLICEMEN have ventured a
few feet out onto the rotten boards. They are trying to hook
something with a long stick (the tramp's bag).

From the catwalk, JOHN, one of the policemen, holds up the
tramp's bag.

SERGEANT
Oi! What are you doing? What you got?

JOHN
(shouts)
Bag!

MICHAEL
It's the man's bag.

SERGEANT
Right.

JOHN
(shouts)
Here. He went in here!

SERGEANT
What the hell was he doing on there?

MICHAEL
Looking.

SERGEANT
He was what, Michael?

MICHAEL
Looking. He was looking in the water.

SERGEANT
You reckon? Well, you might be right. But there
ain't much to look at, is there?
(shouts)
John! See if you can find his hat!

JOHN
(shouts)
What?

SERGEANT
Look for a hat.

JOHN
Right.

The FROGMAN beneath the water indicates he has found the
body.

SERGEANT
Right. They got the bugger, they got him. Now,
Mr Wyatt, I ain't too happy about this. Not happy
at all.

BARRY WYATT
I had a word with him. He says he wants to have a
look.

The SERGEANT sighs.

DOCTOR
It's not pleasant, you know.

SERGEANT
I think you should take him home, get him out of
it. Bloody awful sight – won't do him a mite of
good. None of us. Won't make nobody's day.

The POLICEMEN in the dinghy pass the end of the line to the
FROGMAN who dives back under the surface of the water.

DOCTOR
How many days is it, since you saw him alive?

BARRY WYATT
At least a week.

DOCTOR
Can't you whisk the lad off home, put your foot
down? It's not going to be pleasant for him.

BARRY WYATT
Right. Michael, come here. They're bringing the
body out now.

MICHAEL
I know.

BARRY WYATT
Sergeant and the doctor seen this kind of thing
before; they reckon you ought not to stay.

MICHAEL
Do I have to go?

BARRY WYATT
No, you don't have to if you don't want to.

                MICHAEL
I want to stay.

                BARRY WYATT
Alright, fair enough. He wants to stay.

                SERGEANT
Alright . . . bugger it.

The SERGEANT walks down to the water's edge and calls to
the TWO POLICEMEN who are searching the ground over by
the catwalk.

                SERGEANT
Malcolm . . .

He waves them over.

                DOCTOR
                (to MICHAEL)
Michael, when a body has been a week under
water it can begin to decompose – go rotten. It
may not, but . . . I've seen it before and I don't
like it very much, and I'm sure you won't like it
either. Are you sure you want to stay? If you want
to stay you can, but do say when you've had
enough.

With the help of the FROGMEN they haul in the TRAMP's
body. Once ashore a POLICEMAN detaches the cord from the
body. The DOCTOR makes his inspection.

                DOCTOR
He's remarkably well-preserved for a week under
water – the water must be very clean. Get them in
warm water, especially if there's effluence about,
they blow up in no time. A little discolouration at
the root of the neck. Rigor has passed off. Bottom
two buttons of the overcoat are undone. Fly
button undone.

SERGEANT
Having a piss and fell in. Silly bugger, that's what he done.

DOCTOR
I would say it was an accident, but . . . he did not die by drowning.

SERGEANT
How did he go then?

DOCTOR
Asphyxia. There is no water in the lungs. Shock causes a spasm in the throat muscles, water cannot enter the lungs. It's an unusual case, we'll have to do a post mortem.
(to MICHAEL)
Satisfied?

MICHAEL nods his head.

SERGEANT
Right boys, take him away.
(shouts)
John! Malcolm! Finished – home!

DOCTOR
(To BARRY WYATT)
I've seen worse.

MICHAEL
How long does it take?

DOCTOR
What?

MICHAEL
Drowning. How long does it take before you're dead?

DOCTOR
Oh, not long.

MICHAEL
How long?

DOCTOR
Five minutes in fresh water, in salt water, in the
sea, it can take ten.

BARRY WYATT
I didn't know that. Why's that then?

DOCTOR
Blood is thicker than water, in fresh water that is.
Water goes into the lungs and is then drawn into
the bloodstream, so you get blood dilution – the
blood turns to water. Salt water is thicker than
blood, so the process is reversed. Fluid is drawn
from the blood – you get blood concentration. It
takes longer to die that way.

MICHAEL
Why do they blow up?

DOCTOR
Swell up, not blow up.

MICHAEL
Oh . . .

DOCTOR
Germs in the stomach generate gas and the body
swells up. If the water's warm and dirty they will
probably blow up.

MICHAEL
What would have happened if he'd stayed in there
a long time?

DOCTOR
He'd disappear – rot. Just leave a few old bones
lying about the place.

MICHAEL
Would that happen to me if I drowned?

DOCTOR
It would happen to all of us. None of us is
different in that respect.

MICHAEL
Is it something to be afraid of?

DOCTOR
Dying?

BARRY WYATT
Well, if you're afraid, if you worry about it all the
time, you can't live, can you?

MICHAEL
I wasn't afraid of being born, was I?

47   Int. Courtroom. Day.   47

HEALEY cross-examines LAURA WYATT.

HEALEY
Miss Wyatt, if you had not been dyslexic, if you
had been a perfectly normal, happy child, would
you still be able to say you have received an
efficient full-time and suitable education?

LAURA
Yes. I would.

HEALEY
Apart from motor mechanics, roofing, painting
and decorating, and so on, you learned to thatch
when you were fourteen – is that correct?

LAURA
I started when I was fourteen.

HEALEY
Yes, it must have taken a considerable amount of
time.

LAURA
It does.

HEALEY
Looking back, do you not wish your parents had
guided you to some more relevant activity –
reading and writing, for example?

LAURA
I did not learn to thatch at the expense of my
reading and writing. Quite the reverse, in fact.

HEALEY
Thatching is hardly a pre-requisite for life in our
modern, industrial society, is it?

LAURA
Frankly, I do not think it is for you to judge
whether my interest in thatching is relevant or not
– my parents did not set out to educate us so that
we could find jobs in industry.

HEALEY
You did not learn to read and write until you were
sixteen years of age, is that correct?

LAURA
That is correct.

HEALEY
But you can read now.

LAURA
Yes.

HEALEY
If I gave you something to read now, an article in
this magazine for example, would you be able to
read it?

LAURA
Yes. I have just said I can read.

HEALEY
Very well, could I ask you to read this article to the court?

LAURA
I am not very good at reading aloud.

HEALEY
You cannot read aloud.

LAURA
I find it difficult.

HEALEY
But you can read.

LAURA
Yes.

HEALEY
If you read the article to yourself, would you understand what you had read?

LAURA
What is the article about?

HEALEY
It is about cooking.

LAURA
I can cook so I'd probably understand it.

HEALEY
Very well, could I ask you to look at the article?

The magazine is passed to LAURA. She looks over it.

HEALEY
Do you understand the article?

LAURA
Yes.

HEALEY
What is the article about?

LAURA

. . . Cooking.

HEALEY

Yes, I told you the article is about cooking: are you
able to go into a little detail?

LAURA

Yes, I am.

HEALEY

Then will you please do so?

LAURA

No.

HEALEY

Perhaps we are at cross purposes. Are you
refusing to tell the court what you have read about
in the article?

LAURA

Yes, I am.

HEALEY

What is your reason?

LAURA

You are trying to test me. I do not wish to be
tested.

HEALEY

This is not a test; I simply wish to establish if you
are able to read or not.

LAURA

I can read. I have told you I can read.

JUDGE WOOD

The request is reasonable, Miss Wyatt. Mr Healey
simply wishes to establish your basic level of
reading comprehension. We might then go on to
ask how you have achieved this.

LAURA
I have said that I can read, Your Honour.

JUDGE WOOD
You cannot read aloud.

LAURA
I find it difficult.

JUDGE WOOD
So how are we to know how well you can read?

LAURA
I can read well.

JUDGE WOOD
Then you have nothing to fear. Please answer
Mr Healey's question.

HEALEY
Miss Wyatt, can you please tell the court, and
please refer to the magazine if you so wish to,
what is the article you have before you about?

LAURA WYATT reads the magazine article.

As she reads, she begins to shake. There are tears in her eyes
which she tries to hold back.

LAURA
This is an article explaining a diet which does not
involve cooking. It says, 'The Cook-Free Diet is
fresh, fruity and fun. The chip pan fry-up is a
thing of the past.' It explains that fruit and
vegetables provide most of our vitamin C, half our
vitamin A, some B Complex, E and K. 'To get the
most from your vegetables, buy them farm-fresh
and crunchy . . . never when they're wilting.
Following this kind of diet a person can lose up to
six pounds in the first week and an average of two
and a half pounds a week after that . . . A super
summer diet to bring you and your man down to
size' . . . is that what you want?

Part Three

48   Ext. Lincolnshire. Day.   48

The flat Lincolnshire landscape. Black fields. It is raining.

In the distance, at the end of the track, a FIGURE carrying an umbrella walks towards the Wyatt's home.

49   Int. Workshop. Day.   49

MICHAEL lights the flame on the welder.

50   Ext. Yard. Day.   50

JUDGE WOOD, appropriately dressed for the country, arrives at the house. He looks round the yard then walks towards the workshop.

51   Int. Workshop. Day.   51

The dinghy is in the process of repair.

MICHAEL is welding a join on the bottom of the boat. His concentration is broken by the arrival of JUDGE WOOD. He turns off the welder and lifts the face guard.

>   JUDGE WOOD
> Good afternoon.

MICHAEL says nothing; he continues his work. JUDGE WOOD is not easily put off.

>   JUDGE WOOD
> Michael.

>   MICHAEL
> That's right.

JUDGE WOOD
I am from the court.

MICHAEL
I know.

JUDGE WOOD
Good. Your mother and father are in court for failing to send you to a proper school. I suppose you know that too. I'm here to see what you can do, and where you do it. My name is Wood.

MICHAEL
I know.

JUDGE WOOD
. . . And you're Michael.

MICHAEL
I know.

JUDGE WOOD
I hope this is not going to be a sullen occasion. Your parents are not here today, are they?

MICHAEL
No.

JUDGE WOOD
You see, I know something too.

MICHAEL
Do you want a conducted tour?

JUDGE WOOD
No, thank you.

MICHAEL
There's loads to see if you want.

JUDGE WOOD
I'm sure. Is that what your mother said?

MICHAEL
She told me to tell you to help yourself.

JUDGE WOOD
I'm fine, thank you, Michael. I'm just here to tag
along with you. Follow the child . . . as your
mother says. Where is Laura?

MICHAEL
She's plumbing a house down the road.

JUDGE WOOD
What are you doing to the boat?

MICHAEL
I've welded this join. There was a leak along here.
It's alright now though. My welding is still a bit
rough.

JUDGE WOOD
O yes, welding – most interesting.

MICHAEL
Sit over there, if you want.

JUDGE WOOD
You carry on, Michael.

MICHAEL
I am.

JUDGE WOOD sits on a box. MICHAEL turns on the portable
grinder.

There is a small explosion in the plugtop and the portable
grinder stops.

MICHAEL
Bugger.

JUDGE WOOD
What is wrong?

MICHAEL
The bloody thing is always blowing fuses, there's
something wrong with it.

JUDGE WOOD
Do you swear a lot?

> MICHAEL
> Not much – do you?

> JUDGE WOOD
> Only on occasion. Is it your boat?

> MICHAEL
> Me and dad built it in the summer.

> JUDGE WOOD
> And now it's full of holes.

> MICHAEL
> No it's not.

52 **Ext. Yard. Day.** **52**

Having carried the boat across the yard, JUDGE WOOD and MICHAEL struggle to load it into the back of the Morris Commercial van. They drop it.

> JUDGE WOOD
> That need not have happened.

53 **Ext. Yard. Day.** **53**

Starting the van: MICHAEL at the starting handle, JUDGE WOOD with his foot on the throttle. MICHAEL swings the handle once – it doesn't start. He walks round and leans into the van to check the choke.

> MICHAEL
> Keep your foot half-way down.

> JUDGE WOOD
> That's what I'm doing Michael.

MICHAEL swings the handle and the engine starts.

> MICHAEL
> (yelling)
> Take your foot off. Take your foot off.

MICHAEL runs round and gets his hand on the accelerator.

> MICHAEL
> Move over. Mind the gear stick.

JUDGE WOOD moves into the passenger seat, MICHAEL gets into the driver's seat. JUDGE WOOD has a constant urge to interfere, to do things his own way.

> JUDGE WOOD
> Where are we going?

> MICHAEL
> I'll show you.

> JUDGE WOOD
> I'm sure, but that doesn't answer my question.

> MICHAEL
> You want to come?

> JUDGE WOOD
> Are you planning to take this vehicle on the highway?

> MICHAEL
> How can I? It's not taxed and there's no MOT.

MICHAEL pushes in the choke, engages first, and drives the van out of the yard and down the track.

54   Ext. Track. Day.   54

A rough track leading to the gravel pit. Puddles and heavy mud.

The van rattles along the track with MICHAEL at the wheel.

55   Ext. Gravel Pit. Day.   55

MICHAEL reverses the van towards the edge of the gravel pit. The ground is soft, wet and muddy. The wheels begin to spin and sink down towards the van's axle. They get out of the van.

> MICHAEL
> It won't go any further.

> JUDGE WOOD
> Don't let that concern you, Michael. It's a miracle we've got this far.

MICHAEL opens the back of the van.

> JUDGE WOOD
> I presume you are intending to launch this thing.

They pull the boat out of the van, drag it down to the water's edge.

---

56   Ext. Gravel Pit. Day.   56

MICHAEL sits in the centre of the boat; JUDGE WOOD sits at the stern facing MICHAEL.

The boat floats, motionless, in the centre of the gravel pit.

> MICHAEL
> We're sitting on top of thirty feet of water.

> JUDGE WOOD
> Really?

> MICHAEL
> Do you want to take a look?

> JUDGE WOOD
> I can see, thank you.

MICHAEL offers him the viewing box.

> MICHAEL
> You can use this. You can see right down to the bottom.

> JUDGE WOOD
> I really don't think I should hang over the edge,
> do you?

> MICHAEL
> You'll be alright.

> JUDGE WOOD
> I'm sure. We've taken on a bit of water.

> MICHAEL
> Do you want to carry on? Are you ready?

> JUDGE WOOD
> I thought this was it – where else is there to go?

> MICHAEL
> I want to show you something.

MICHAEL rows directly towards the large reed bed.

> JUDGE WOOD
> We're going to hit the reeds.

> MICHAEL
> I know.

The boat ploughs into the reeds and stops.

As MICHAEL turns to climb to the front of the boat, just a few
yards ahead in the reed bed a heron takes flight.

> MICHAEL
> Look!

They watch the bird fly up and away into the distance.

---

57   Ext. Gravel Pit. Day.   57

On the reed bed: a nest. MICHAEL has battled the boat into
position.

> MICHAEL
> Look, there it is.

The boat tips as MICHAEL moves to get a better view.

> MICHAEL
> Look, really big, isn't it?

> JUDGE WOOD
> What kind of nest is it?

> MICHAEL
> It's a heron's.

> JUDGE WOOD
> Yes, of course, a heron's nest; yes.

> MICHAEL
> This is special, this nest.

MICHAEL leans over the nest and finds a piece of shell and other trophies.

> JUDGE WOOD
> Steady!

> MICHAEL
> Egg shell!

> JUDGE WOOD
> Tell me, Michael, how many species of heron are there in the British Isles?

> MICHAEL
> How many what?

> JUDGE WOOD
> How many kinds of heron?

> MICHAEL
> I don't know.

> JUDGE WOOD
> Is there more than one?

> MICHAEL
> They don't nest in reed beds in England, they nest in trees. Big oak trees.

JUDGE WOOD
What is their wing span?

MICHAEL
Pretty big – they nest in marshes in Holland, but not here, not for a hundred years.

JUDGE WOOD
And we've gone and scared it off . . . for another hundred. Isn't it a bit unusual for a bird to still be on the site, on the nest, at this time of year?

MICHAEL
Do you know about herons?

JUDGE WOOD
No. No, I don't. I'm just drawing on a rather slim store of ornithological knowledge. Very slim. Look here, we're definitely shipping water. It's gushing about in the bottom – we'll soon have more in than out.

MICHAEL
It's not coming in where I mended it.

JUDGE WOOD
Does that matter? My God, there's the spot. It's gushing in!

MICHAEL
There's a duckboard missing. I bet you did it when you jumped into the boat.

JUDGE WOOD
Does it really matter? Jumped? Michael, I think we should head for the shore. Michael, we're taking on water in considerable quantities.

MICHAEL
It's alright, we're safe.

JUDGE WOOD has had enough. He takes one of the oars and begins to paddle for the shore.

> JUDGE WOOD
> The sodding thing is sinking.

Thinking of the thirty feet of water, JUDGE WOOD rows harder, trying to push the boat out of the reed bank.

> JUDGE WOOD
> The sodding thing is sinking!

> MICHAEL
> It doesn't really matter.

> JUDGE WOOD
> We're going down fast.

> MICHAEL
> It's very shallow here. That's why the reeds grow on this side.

> JUDGE WOOD
> We're sinking.

The boat is stuck several yards from the bank. JUDGE WOOD and MICHAEL stand as the boat slowly fills with water and sinks down to the bottom of the pit. They wait until it settles on the bottom.

> JUDGE WOOD
> It's cold.

> MICHAEL
> We'll have to wade.

> JUDGE WOOD
> Yes.

MICHAEL climbs out of the front of the boat and stands in no more than nine inches of water. JUDGE WOOD climbs out of the back of the boat and goes in up to his knees.
They wade to the bank. JUDGE WOOD finds the going difficult. He steps into a rather deep hole beneath the water and stumbles. He is soaked. When he stands, his trousers are full of water.

Once out of the pit.

>JUDGE WOOD
>Oh blast! God!

>MICHAEL
>Are you angry?

>JUDGE WOOD
>Yes. Quite angry.

58   Ext. Gravel Pit. Day.   58

JUDGE WOOD and MICHAEL make their way round the edge of the gravel pit back towards the van.

It is slow, heavy work on the muddy ground, particularly for JUDGE WOOD.

59   Ext. Gravel Pit. Day.   59

MICHAEL closes the back doors of the van. JUDGE WOOD is tired, wet and cold. He sits in the passenger seat. MICHAEL gets into the driver's seat.

>JUDGE WOOD
>Do you . . . want my foot on the throttle?

>MICHAEL
>No, we've warmed her up, she should start on her own.

>JUDGE WOOD
>How do you propose to move this vehicle when the back axle is in six feet of mud?

>MICHAEL
>I'll have a go.

>JUDGE WOOD
>I'm sure you will.

MICHAEL pulls the starter. The engine groans once and then ceases to function. MICHAEL pulls the starter again – nothing.

He tries for a third time. Nothing.

> JUDGE WOOD
> What's the matter?

> MICHAEL
> The starter motor's seized up. We need spanners and a hammer.

> JUDGE WOOD
> Have you got them?

> MICHAEL
> No.

> JUDGE WOOD
> Where's the crank?

> MICHAEL
> Back at the yard.

> JUDGE WOOD
> (the anger and frustration coming right to the surface)
> You're making quite a day of it, aren't you?

> MICHAEL
> Don't worry –

> JUDGE WOOD
> You're really having a day.

> MICHAEL
> It doesn't matter.

> JUDGE WOOD
> You've blown up the workshop.

> MICHAEL
> It was only the fuse.

JUDGE WOOD
Fuses blown. You have destroyed and virtually
sunk this monstrosity!
(indicating the van)

MICHAEL
We'll soon sort it out.

JUDGE WOOD
(looking straight on)
You've certainly sunk the boat. Do you realize we
could have drowned, boy. Do you hear?
Drowned. You could have drowned us both. Dear
God! I'm soaked to the – and the bloody motor
starter's stuck!

MICHAEL
We only bought the van to keep chickens in and
it's been going for three years.

JUDGE WOOD
Chickens! Is this all part of a normal day?

MICHAEL
No.

JUDGE WOOD
Creative learning. Follow the child. My God, how
would it be following fifteen hundred children in
the average comprehensive? I think you're for the
high jump, boy.

MICHAEL
Pardon?

JUDGE WOOD
Have you sunk the boat before? Is it a habit?

MICHAEL
No. It wasn't the bit I mended.

JUDGE WOOD
You are for the high jump.

MICHAEL
I don't know what you mean.

JUDGE WOOD
I mean your father, your old man, is going to put a
boot to your backside when he sees this.

MICHAEL
No.

JUDGE WOOD
That is what I mean.

They both stop. JUDGE WOOD is shivering. The sound of
voices in the distance.

Further up the track some SCHOOL CHILDREN accompanied
by TWO TEACHERS are heading towards the gravel pit. They
are on a nature walk.

MICHAEL
Look, they might give us a shove. They came
down here before.

JUDGE WOOD
Children on a nature walk? They couldn't fix a
starter motor, could they? Duffers. We don't have
to go back down the track, do we, Michael? There
must be a short cut back to the house.

MICHAEL
Across the field.

JUDGE WOOD
Good.

60   **Ext. Gravel Pit. Day.**   60

The SCHOOL TEACHER stops the children.

TEACHER
Now listen, before we go any further, I don't want
you in a big clump so you can't see anything –
right. David, what are you doing?

DAVID
I got mud on me, sir.

TEACHER
That's because it's wet – now get back in.

61   **Ext. Field. Day.**   **61**

It is raining. A ploughed field: heavy, black earth.

MICHAEL in front. JUDGE WOOD trails – he becomes
increasingly fatigued as they trek across the muddy field.

JUDGE WOOD
What are you going to do, eh?

MICHAEL
I don't know.

JUDGE WOOD
'Don't know'? Ought to know.

MICHAEL
Why are you trying to frighten me?

JUDGE WOOD
What are you going to do if you want to be a
doctor or a solicitor? What are you going to do?
How are you going to get your qualifications?

MICHAEL
You mean exams?

JUDGE WOOD
I mean exams. If you want to make something of
your life you'll have to pass exams.

MICHAEL
Did you take lots of exams?

JUDGE WOOD
Yes I did.

MICHAEL
Did you pass them all?

JUDGE WOOD
Yes I did.

MICHAEL
What if you hadn't passed them?

JUDGE WOOD
Then I'd have been a duffer and I wouldn't be
where I am today. Clifton, Balliol. Second in
History. First in Law. Queen's Counsel, onto the
Bench. Honorary Fellow, Balliol. President,
Clifton. British Member to the Permanent Court of
Arbitration at the Hague and I didn't get any of
that sitting around waiting for the urge to read to
strike me.

He stops. Total fatigue. He can't move. Skin turned to clay.

JUDGE WOOD
Michael . . .

MICHAEL stops and turns. He looks at JUDGE WOOD for some
time. JUDGE WOOD cannot move. The rain is pelting down.

JUDGE WOOD
Michael . . .

He cannot ask for help.

JUDGE WOOD
(pointing to himself)
Tired.

62   Int. Kitchen. Day.   62

JUDGE WOOD sits in the kitchen in front of the Aga.

MICHAEL comes in from the bathroom.

MICHAEL
It's ready.

> JUDGE WOOD
> Yes, thank you.

JUDGE WOOD goes into the bathroom and closes the door.

MICHAEL fills a kettle and puts it onto the Aga. He gets a mug, a lemon, some honey and a bottle of whiskey. He goes into the bathroom.

> MICHAEL
> Give me your clothes, I'll stick them on the Aga.

> JUDGE WOOD
> Yes.

Again, JUDGE WOOD closes the bathroom door. MICHAEL makes a hot drink for him, pouring in liberal quantities of whiskey.

63   Ext. House. Day.   63

Dusk.

MICHAEL stands outside the front door scraping mud from Judge Wood's shoes.

64   Int. Bathroom. Day.   64

JUDGE WOOD is in the bath.

MICHAEL is sitting on a bathroom stool next to the bath. JUDGE WOOD tastes the drink.

> MICHAEL
> Alright?

> JUDGE WOOD
> Very acceptable.

> MICHAEL
> I've hung your clothes on the Aga – they're pretty wet.

MICHAEL quite openly stares at JUDGE WOOD in the bath.

> MICHAEL
> I've put some Radox in there.

> JUDGE WOOD
> Do you normally do this – stare at people in the bath? I believe it is customary in most houses to leave people to take a bath in private.

> MICHAEL
> I often talk to people in the bath. I talk to dad in the bath.

> JUDGE WOOD
> I am not dad.

> MICHAEL
> You've got blue lumps on your legs – you're old, aren't you?

> JUDGE WOOD
> Well, I'm not exactly teetering on the edge of the pit. Not just yet.

> MICHAEL
> Do you expect to die soon?

> JUDGE WOOD
> I think I'm good for a few years yet, thank you. This is a most unpleasant line of questioning – can we not pick a less enervating topic?

> MICHAEL
> Are you my friend?

> JUDGE WOOD
> What do you make of all this fuss, Michael? Countless officials and experts expensively involved, trying to get you into school, just so that you can read, write, and do your sums. What is to be done, eh? You can't read a dicky, can you? The three Rs. Where else is one to begin? Where? How old are you, Michael?

MICHAEL
Eleven.

JUDGE WOOD
Eleven. When I was eleven, my father took a
diplomatic post in the East – the Middle East
actually – and I was packed up and sent off to
boarding school here, in England. I didn't like it
very much and I cried quite a lot. It wasn't that
tough. Not really. I am not here to hurt you,
Michael, or your feelings. Every child has the right
to read, write, and do their numbers. It is not a
punishment to be sent to school and learn how to
read, do you know? It is your right, hard fought
for and won. I am here to protect your rights,
Michael – I am here as your friend.

65   Int. Courtroom. Day.   65

CLERK OF THE COURT
Be upstanding in court.

Everybody in the courtroom stands, including the WYATTS.
JUDGE WOOD enters the courtroom and sits in his chair.

JUDGE WOOD
In giving judgement in this case, let me say at the
outset that we do not think we are dealing here
with parents who are in any way indifferent to the
education of their children. These are not parents
who are prepared to let their children play truant
from school on the specious excuse they will learn
as much at home. They are responsible and caring
people who are trying to give their children a
proper upbringing to fit them for adult life. The
appellants in this case are guilty of the offences of
which they were charged in the Magistrates Court
unless they prove they were at the material time
causing their child to 'receive efficient full-time

education suitable to his age, ability and aptitude, otherwise than in school'. There is no definitions section in the Education Act. Thus, relevant words such as 'efficient' and, most importantly, 'education' are not given a definition in law. Also, there are no legal precedents to which we might turn for enlightenment. Therefore, since Parliament in drafting the Education Act did not see fit to define 'education', the definition of education is not a matter of fact, but of opinion. The burden of proof, in this case, is on a balance of probabilities only. The appellants' children are, and have been, allowed to follow their own interests and to investigate subjects largely of their own choice without restriction. They have not, however, simply been left to their own devices. Through the example of Laura, and Michael, we are satisfied that for *these* children, their manner of education has proved efficient. They are mature, confident, well-mannered, at ease in all sorts of company. They are lively-minded and have a wide range of practical skills. In our judgement, however, the academic skills of reading, writing and arithmetic are fundamental to any efficient education for life in the modern world. These attainments are essential for communication, research, or self-education. The sooner they are acquired, the greater the advantage of the acquirer. We do not think it proper to reject any attempt to achieve literacy through ordered and systematic application as a source of harm, as the appellants appear to think. Michael's problem of coping with the basic skills of reading and writing *must* be dealt with, and it is our judgement that no real or adequate attention is being paid to it . . .

66   Ext. Gravel Pit. Day.   66

MICHAEL is standing at the end of the catwalk looking out over the water. He has a bag with him.

BARRY WYATT is standing on the bank behind him.

MICHAEL picks up his bag and walks towards his father. They walk off together across the field.

67   Ext. Day.   67

A heron flying in the sky.

68   Ext. School. Day.   68

The school building. The singing of 'All Things Bright and Beautiful' can be heard through this and the following scenes.

69   Int. Classroom. Day.   69

An empty classroom in the school.

We take in the detail of the classroom: blackboard, tables, chairs, etc., to be seen in a detached manner. On the wall there are some 'nature' charts. There is a chart showing trees. Another chart showing a fresh water fish, including the pike. And finally, a rather dilapidated 'bird' chart. We focus on the picture of the heron.

70   Int. Assembly Hall. Day.   70

We move down the rows of singing CHILDREN to see that they are standing in ordered lines.

Then we move along the rows of faces until we reach MICHAEL.

MICHAEL is holding a hymn book. He is the only person who is not singing.

Appendix

The list below gives all but the very minor differences between the text in this book and the broadcast version of the film. The following passages are *not* found in the broadcast version:

Scene 15. Walker: 'Was she in' *to* Wyatt: 'She was fine.'
Scene 26. Wyatt: 'You think she's' *to* 'Laura knows who they are talking about.'
Harper: 'Such decisions . . . could not allow it.'
Scene 27. This is not in the broadcast version.
Scene 28. Wood: '"or otherwise"' *to* Spencer: 'the local authority.'
Wood: 'If you are . . . child to school.'
Spencer: 'How long has she' *to* Wyatt: 'she's now eighteen.'

Scene 31. Spencer: 'Your Honour, Dr Margaret Powell . . . to be necessary.'
Spencer: 'It will be evident . . . No, Your Honour.'
Scene 33. Spencer: 'What do you mean' *to* Wyatt: 'a different story.' though 3 lines from this passage are in the broadcast version.
Scene 36. Wyatt: 'First, we concentrate' *to* Healey: 'the average school.'
Wyatt: 'Whereas a school . . . finds difficult'.
Wyatt: 'The best way . . . is experience.'
Healey: 'If they set . . . is that correct?'
Healey: 'Let us take an example' *to* Wyatt: 'do with dyslexia.'
Wyatt: 'It takes time . . . Not yet.'
Scene 39. Healey: 'Is there any' *to* Wyatt: 'trying to achieve.'
Healey: 'Yes, but what . . . efficient education.'
Scene 45. Wyatt: 'Possibly, in which' *to* Healey: 'to Michael.'

Scene 65. Wood: 'The appellants . . . practical skills.'
Wood: 'These attainments . . . paid to it.'